HOW TO PLAY GUITAR

Table of Contents

This book contains many examples on how to play guitar and there's no better way to learn than hearing the guitar audio clips alongside reading. You can follow along with this book using the guitar audio examples found here:

https://soundcloud.com/jason_randall/sets/how-to-play-guitar-a-beginners-guide-to-learn-how-to-play-the-guitar-audio-examples

Or by searching this book's title in SoundCloud.

CHAPTER 1

Introduction

If you are reading this, you have decided you want to learn how to play the guitar, one of the world's most popular and versatile instruments! This book will teach you everything you need to know to build a solid foundation and begin your musical journey.

A Brief History of the Guitar

Stringed descendants of the guitar such as the lute, renaissance guitar, oud, and vihuela have been around for hundreds of years, but the archetypical 6-string guitar we know and love today began its life in the 1800s when Spanish guitar makers like Antonio de Torres Jurado built what came to be known as the 'classical guitar'. Andrés Segovia (known as the 'grandfather of the classical guitar' did much to popularize and earn respect for this instrument in the early 1900s.

Around the same time in the United States, luthiers like C.F. Martin were creating louder, steel-stringed instruments, known as 'acoustic guitars' that were favored by blues and folk players of the time, while Orville Gibson made guitars that resembled orchestral instruments like the violin, called 'archtop guitars'.

In the 1930's, George Beauchamp designed the first known electrically amplified guitar, known as the 'frying pan' and thus the 'electric guitar' was born. The first mass market electric guitar was the Gibson ES-150, a hollowbody instrument first introduced in 1936. It was the first guitar that could cut through the murk and be heard over the wailing horn sections in big band orchestras of the time, making it the go to guitar for jazzers, as evidenced by its use by none other than virtuoso Charlie Christian. Later models like the ES-250 were used by early electric blues legend T-Bone Walker.

In 1941, Les Paul took a solid block of maple wood and wired a Gibson pickup to it in an effort to reduce feedback. This instrument was known as 'the log' and allowed for guitarists to play at much higher volume than ever before. 'The log' is the first solid-bodied electric guitar which was an essential step in the eventual development of the Gibson 'Les Paul', one of the most iconic electric guitar designs whose endorsers include the likes of Jimmy Page, Slash, Randy Rhoads, Alex Lifeson, Zakk Wylde, and Peter Frampton, to name a few.

The invention of the 'Les Paul' was followed closely in 1954 by what is arguably the most copied and popular guitar design of all time, the Fender 'Stratocaster', designed by Leo Fender. This guitar was unique for its double cutaway body to allow easy access to the higher frets and upper range of the instrument, its 3 pickups and 3-way (and eventually 5-way) selector switch which allowed the player a variety of tones, and its floating bridge and whammy/ tremolo arm which allowed the player to lower or raise the pitch of all 6 strings or apply vibrato (this was later taken to the extreme by Jimi Hendrix who used the whammy bar to create stunning 'dive bomb' effects and wild feedback drenched harmonic squeals).

The next big development in guitar history came when Link Wray accidentally discovered a way to overdrive the vacuum tubes in his amplifier, giving the guitar a dirty, distorted tone and becoming a part of his signature sound on his breakthrough hit "Rumble" (he was able to achieve even more distortion by poking holes in the speakers). To recreate this hugely popular sound and to save guitarists the trouble of doing irreparable damage to their hard earned equipment, Gibson created the Maestro FZ-1 Fuzz-Tone stompbox, the worlds first mass produced 'effects pedal'. Thanks to this revolutionary device, today's guitarists can colour their sound in countless ways with effects like chorus, delay, wah-wah, fuzz, phaser, and much more.

Given the versatility of tone, as well as the ability to play melodically as a lead instrument (one note at a time), or harmonically as a rhythmic instrument (2 or more notes at a time) the guitar has become a mainstay in almost every style of music, and there's something out there for everyone!

Hopefully you can now appreciate how far the guitar has come to get into your hands. There has never been a better time to learn. Let's get to it!

CHAPTER 2

Guitar Anatomy 101

Topics covered:

- Parts of the guitar and what they look like

- How guitars work

- Tuning your guitar

Can't tell your headstock from your lower bout? Wondering what all those knobs and switches do? Can't tell if a certain guitar is acoustic or electric? This chapter will help you learn the parts of the guitar, what they do, and what they look like.

Parts of the Guitar

Acoustic and electric guitars are essentially the same instrument and share a lot of the same parts, but each has its unique components, which we will specify with the symbol (a) for acoustic and (e) for electric.

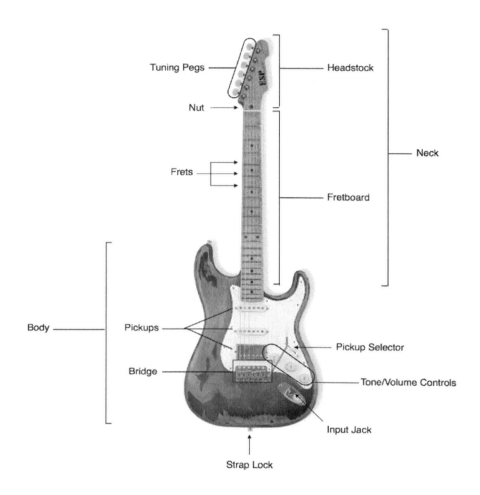

Tuning Pegs — Headstock

Nut →

Frets

Neck

Fretboard

Body — Pickups

Pickup Selector

Bridge

Tone/Volume Controls

Input Jack

Strap Lock

Body: This is the largest section of the guitar and is responsible for the resonance and overall tone of the instrument. Depending on the type of guitar, bodies are either *solid, hollow,* or *semi-hollow.* Guitar bodies come in all shapes and sizes and are made mostly of wood, but also come in aluminium, plastic, and even cardboard. Being the largest part of the guitar, the body itself contains a number of smaller parts including the bridge, pickguard, volume pots (e), pickups (e), and input jack (e).

Bridge: Located on the lower bout (or lower half) of the guitar body, the bridge acts as an anchor for the strings. On acoustic guitars, these are made of wood, while on electric they are made of metal. Electric guitar bridges can be hard-tail (or non-vibrato) meaning the pitch cannot be actively controlled, or floating (vibrato) which allows the player to raise or lower the pitch of the strings by using a lever which is known as a whammy-bar or tremolo arm.

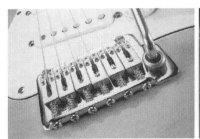

Cutaway: An indent or two (single vs. double cutaway) in the upper bout of the guitar designed to grant easier access to the higher frets. This is a distinctive feature of most electric guitars, but can also be found on acoustic guitars.

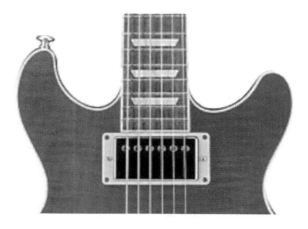

Frets: The metal wires that lie on the fretboard, perpendicular to the strings. When the string is depressed behind the fret, the length is effectively shortened and a unique pitch is produced. The closer to the bridge you get, the higher the fret number, the shorter the string length and therefore the higher the pitch (and vice versa).

Fretboard: A plank of wood attached to the neck in which the *frets* are embedded. This is also called the *fingerboard* as it is the main point of contact for your fretting hand fingers.

The **Headstock** the uppermost part of the guitar, located at the end of the *neck*, above the *nut* and *fretboard*, where the *tuning posts* hold the strings in place. This is also the part where the guitar manufacturer's name is displayed, and each model has its own distinctive shape.

Neck: Another major part of the guitar connected the body, on which the *fretboard* lies. Necks can be carved out of the same piece of wood as the body (neck-through) or more commonly, be a separate piece altogether which is bolted on or glued to the body.

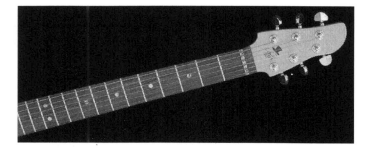

The **Nut** is a grooved piece of bone, plastic, or metal through which the strings pass, separating the *fretboard* from the *headstock*. It is essentially fret number 0, and all frets are numbered relative to the nut.

Pickups (e) are basically like a microphone for the electric guitar. They consist of a coil of copper wire wrapped around a magnet (one per string) and typically housed inside a plastic or metal covering. When a string is plucked, the magnetic field of the pickup is disturbed, creating magnetic flux which is then transmitted through a cable and converted into sound when it reaches an amplifier, producing a pitch. Pickups come in a variety of styles and are typically either single-coil or humbuckers, each with their own unique sound.

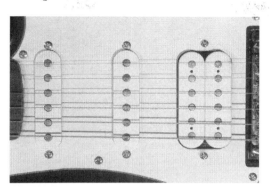

Pickup selector (e): A switch that allows you to select which *pickup* the vibration of the strings is transmitted through. This can alter the tone of an electric guitar significantly.

Strap Locks are pegs upon which a strap can be fastened to facilitate playing while standing and to aid in adjusting the height of the guitar to a desired level.

Strings are arguably the most important part of the guitar and the reason every other part of the guitar is there, because they are responsible for producing the sound! They are made of nylon or steel (and at one time, cat gut), and a standard guitar has 6 of them, though up to 12 string variations of the guitar exist. Technically they are not a permanent part of the guitar since they are replaceable and often break (if you can invent a permanent unbreakable string, take my money).

Tuning pegs are used to raise or lower the desired pitch of each string by rotation, thereby tuning the strings. The pegs are attached to the headstock in one row of six or two rows of three (on a typical 6 string guitar).

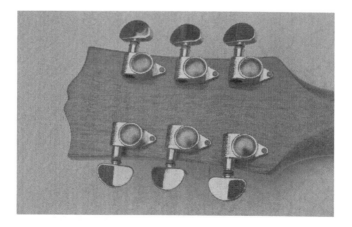

Tone/volume controls are also known as "pots" or potentiometers that control the amount of output of certain parameters of sound. The volume pot rather obviously controls the volume, typically from 0-10 (though some guitars might go to 11!), 0 being no output and 10 being full output. Tone controls add bass and subtract treble on one end and add treble and subtract bass on the other, with 0 being the most 'bassy' and 10 being the most 'trebly', sort of like a mini wah-wah pedal.

How Guitars Work

All instruments require some form of vibration to move the air around them and a produce a sound in a consistent and controllable frequency. The human voice uses vibrating vocal cords, the saxophone uses vibrating reeds, and stringed instruments like the violin, banjo and guitar use, well, vibrating strings!

Plucking, or setting a string on the guitar in motion causes it to vibrate and produce a pitch. The more tense the string, the higher the pitch. The less tense the string, the lower the pitch (think about stretching and plucking a rubber band).

To change the pitch of a guitar string, we can turn the *tuning pegs* one way or the other to increase or decrease the tension, or we can alter the LENGTH of a string. Since the strings are of a set length, it is impossible to lengthen them, but it is possible to shorten them. In order to shorten the string, we press the string down on the *frets* of the guitar. The higher UP the neck (toward the bridge) you fret a string, the higher pitch, and vice versa.

So, pitch is achieved by shortening the strings on the guitar, this is why mandolins and ukuleles sound higher pitched than the guitar.

Electric guitars use magnetic *pickups* to convert the vibration of the strings into an electrical signal which then passes through an *amplifier* and is turned into sound waves when it is output through a loudspeaker.

An **acoustic** guitar guitar produces its sound acoustically, and the vibrating strings transmit sound waves through the *body* which resonate in the cavity of the guitar and out through the *sound hole,* just like the vibrations from your vocal cords resonate in the cavity of your mouth and exit through your lips.

THEORY NOTE: In Western music, the *octave* is divided into 12 equal parts, meaning there are only 12 unique notes from which to choose (A A#/Bb B C C#/Db D D#/Eb E F F#/Gb G G#/Ab). This is called the *chromatic scale.* The shortest distance or *interval* between notes is called a *semitone* or 1/2 tone. On the guitar, a *semitone* is the distance between two adjacent frets (on the same string).

Tuning

Each string of the guitar is numbered from 1 to 6, with 1 being the skinniest and highest pitched string and 6 being the thickest and lowest pitched string. In 'standard tuning' (the most common way to tune a guitar) the guitar is tuned as follows:

1st string = **E**

2nd string = **B**

3rd string = **G**

4th string = **D**

5th string = **A**

6th string = **E**

Typically, we guitarists express this from the lowest sounding string to the highest sounding string which looks like:

E A D G B E

Some beginning players find it helpful to express this in a mnemonic such as "**E**ddie **A**te **D**ynamite. **G**ood**B**ye **E**ddie!"

It is highly recommended that you purchase an electronic tuner or if you have a smart phone, download a tuning app. There are many free options to chose from and it is an essential accessory.

PRO TIP: The first thing EVERY GUITARIST, regardless of skill, should do before sitting down to practice, take a lesson, or play a gig is TUNE THE GUITAR!

If you don't have a tuner handy you can tune by ear, though this requires practice. If there is another in-tune instrument like a piano nearby (and you or a friend know the note names) you can try and match the pitch of each string to said instrument. So, start by tuning the 6th string by playing an E on the piano and using the tuning pegs on your guitar to make it match that pitch. Do this for every string.

Another popular method of tuning by ear is to use the '**5th fret trick**' in which, assuming your 6th string is in tune, you match each open string's pitch to the pitch of the 5th fret of the adjacent string below it in pitch.

Don't worry, it's easier done than said! To put it simply. The 5th fret of the low **E** string (6th string) should sound the exact same as the open **A** string, as they are both A notes (if you play the 5th fret of the E string and the A doesn't match, you need to turn the tuning knob of the A string until it does). Apply the same to the other strings like so:

The 5th fret of the **A** string should sound like the open **D** string.

The 5th fret of the **D** string should sound like the open **G** string.

The **4th fret** of the **G** string should sound like the open **B** string.

The 5th fret of the **B** string should sound like the open **E** string.

*Note that we use the 4th fret instead of the 5th fret when tuning the **B** string.

This diagram illustrates the 5th fret trick to tuning:

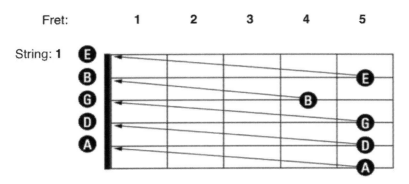

To sum it up, tuning is very important and it is strongly advised that you get yourself a tuner.

Now you know the important parts of the guitar and how the instrument works. You know the difference between an electric and acoustic guitar, and how to tune it. If you don't already have a guitar, the next chapter is just for you!

Play: 1. Tuning
https://soundcloud.com/jason_randall/sets/how-to-play-guitar-a-beginners-guide-to-learn-how-to-play-the-guitar-audio-examples

CHAPTER 3

Buying a Guitar

Topics covered:

- Types of guitar and features

- What to look for

- Popular models and brands

- Choosing the right instrument for you

So you've decided you want to play the guitar? Excellent choice! But before you begin your journey, you're going to need an actual guitar to play. Unless you already own a guitar or have a friend or relative who is willing to give you a guitar, you will probably need to throw down some cold hard cash for your own personal axe (slang for 'guitar'). This chapter will tell you everything you need to know about purchasing your first guitar!

Acoustic or Electric?

The first decision you need to make is whether you want an *acoustic* or an *electric* guitar. Though they are essentially the same instrument, there are many notable differences between different types of guitar, and the decision will ultimately come down to personal taste and preference. Here's what you need to know:

Acoustic Guitar

A standard Yamaha steel-string acoustic guitar.

An **acoustic** guitar is any guitar that produces its sound acoustically, using vibrating strings to produce sound waves which resonate in the guitar's *body,* and requires no amplification. They are typically made mostly of wood, though other, synthetic materials are sometimes used. This is the most common type of guitar you will see in the wild.

There are several distinct sub-categories of **acoustic guitar** including the archetypical *steel-string guitar,* the *classical guitar* (sometimes called *nylon-string* guitars)*,* and the *archtop guitar* (which can be fitted with electronics but are acoustic at heart).

Steel-string acoustic guitars, as the name suggests, are strung with steel strings, have a flat top, and produce a bright and loud natural sound. They come in various sizes with names like 'parlor', 'dreadnought' and 'jumbo', and as a general rule, size is directly proportional to overall volume.

These guitars are great for strumming, fingerpicking and accompanying your own, or somebody else's voice, and are most often used for styles like folk, blues, country, bluegrass, and rock.

PROS:

- Extremely portable (no additional equipment to carry!)

- No need to purchase an amplifier, cables, effects, etc.

- Great for solo playing and vocal accompaniment

- Makes playing electric guitar much easier, as the high string tension will build finger strength.

- Members of the opposite sex will think you to be sensitive and deep.

CONS:

- A little tougher on the fingers than electric guitar due to heavier gauge strings, higher string tension and higher action (the height of the strings above the fretboard).

- Invariable timbre. You're pretty much stuck with the natural sound of the acoustic guitar, unlike the electric guitar whose sound can be altered electronically in myriad ways.

- Due to the higher level of skill required to make acoustic guitars vs. electric guitars, cheap acoustic guitars usually sound worse and are much harder to play and keep in tune than their equivalently priced electric counterpart.

- Even your most sincere attempts to learn 'Wonderwall', 'Stairway to Heaven' and 'Wagon Wheel' will be met with derision from your peers.

A nylon-string classical guitar.

Classical or **nylon-string** guitars are similar to steel-string acoustic guitars in overall construction, but differ in several key areas. Like the steel-string guitar, these guitars have a flat top, (though it is of slightly more delicate construction due to the reduced string tension) but instead use nylon strings and have a wider neck and fretboard to facilitate the intricate fretwork required of classical music. The tone produced by classical guitars is much more mellow than the steel-string acoustic, and they are most often played with fingers only and with a more formal posture.

As the name suggests, these guitars are used primarily for playing classical music, but are also prominent in genres like folk, salsa, bossa nova, samba, country, jazz, and even pop. A louder and more durable variation of this type of guitar is also used for playing flamenco music.

PROS:

- Easy on the fingers.

- Good for players with bigger hands.

- Typically less expensive than entry level acoustic guitars.

- Wider neck makes chords easier to play.

CONS:

- Lower overall volume than steel-string guitars.

- Harder access to higher frets.

- Nylon stretches, which means it takes longer for the strings to 'settle' and therefore requires more tuning than steel-string guitars.

A variation of the **steel-string** acoustic guitar is the **archtop** guitar, which are essentially oversized fretted violins, featuring a hollow body with rounded (or 'arch') top and back with '*f*' *holes* carved into the belly. These are mainly used in jazz and blues styles, and their modern incarnations are often fitted with electronic pickups, making them somewhat of a hybrid between acoustic and electric.

The Godin 5th Avenue, one of the more affordable archtop acoustic guitars.

Electric Guitar

The Stratocaster by Fender, a standard solid-body electric guitar.

Electric guitars use magnetic *pickups* to convert the vibration of the strings into an electrical signal which then passes through an *amplifier* and is turned into sound waves when it is output through a loudspeaker. Because the signal is electric, it can be altered extensively and in myriad ways (such as through the use of effects pedals, which we will cover) thus producing a much larger sonic palate than its acoustic counterpart.

Electric guitars vary greatly in terms of style, tone, and construction, and just like acoustic guitars there are several subcategories of electric guitars, including *solid-body, semi-hollow body,* and *hollow-body,* as well as 7, 8, 9 and 12-string variations (the standard being 6-strings).

The versatility of the electric guitar cannot be stressed enough and it is a staple of genres like pop, rock n' roll, blues, indie, jazz, country, punk, heavy metal, and reggae, just to name a few. If you picture yourself bashing out loud, distorted riffs while flames shoot 10 feet into the air, you'd probably be happiest with an electric guitar.

What to Ask

Purchasing your first guitar can be as easy as going to amazon.com and typing in "guitar" but finding the right guitar for you takes some work! For such an investment, it is recommended that you go see a professional. DON'T just buy a the first, cheapest guitar you see online. DO consult an employee at your local music store. They should be able to tell you all about the many different models and how they stack up against one another. You can also usually try out as many guitars you want (as long as you're gentle), and this will help you to find an instrument that feels right to you. Remember, you can always purchase a model for a better price online after you've gone and tried it out in person.

Here are some questions to ASK YOURSELF before heading to the music store:

What style of music do I want to play?

The answer to this will have a huge impact on which guitar you end up choosing. If you only want to play classical music, you need look no further than the nylon string section. Are you a metal head? You're probably gonna want a guitar with at least 2 humbuckers, a locking tremolo system and an amp with lots of overdrive. Do you just wanna strum some chords around the campfire and think that Bob Dylan sold out when he went electric? Get an acoustic guitar. Do you like to rock but also want to dig into some jazz, blues, funk and reggae? A strat-like electric guitar has the versatility you need.

What guitar model looks best to me?

What's your favourite colour? What's your favourite shape? Does your favourite guitarist play a Gibson Flying V? Style matters, pick a guitar you like looking at.

What is my budget?

As a rule, you should NEVER purchase a cheap guitar unless you only plan on using it as a prop. A $100 acoustic guitar on EBay will most likely sound horrible, go out of tune frequently, break easily and be no fun to play. Whether you're purchasing an acoustic guitar or an electric guitar + amplifier, you should be expecting to spend between $300 and $600 for a durable,good quality instrument that will last for years and you can always upgrade to a more expensive, higher quality guitar further on down the road.

Here are some questions to ASK A GUITAR DEALER:

What would you recommend for _____ style?

What models do you have in the ___-___ price range?

What are your best selling models?

What's the difference between _____ and ____?

Can I try that one? (and that one, and that one and that one?)

The most important thing is this: if you don't know something, ask!

New or Used?

Of course, you don't have to buy a guitar straight from the factory or brand new and hot off the music store wall. There are plenty of people out there who, for one reason or the other, decide to sell their guitars and thanks to them, one can find high-quality instruments for a fraction of the sticker price with a little luck.

With sites like reverb.com, eBay, Craigslist, and Kijiji, as well as local Facebook musical instrument buy and sell communities, finding the right used guitar is easier than it has ever been.

THINGS TO LOOK OUT FOR for when buying a used guitar:

Find out how old the guitar is, how extensively it has been played and how many owners the guitar has had.

Get the numbers. Compare the asking price to that of the same unused model and against other similar used models. Having this information will give you an advantage when negotiating price.

Check for any damage. Chips out of the paint job are purely cosmetic, but cracks, hairline fractures, and missing components are more serious issues that should not be overlooked.

Make sure the neck is aligned with the body and properly adjusted. Depress every fret and pluck every string, all of the frets should produce a clear note.

Play the guitar to see that it sounds right and suits you. Can you see yourself falling in love with this instrument? If you don't yet know how to play, bring a friend who does or ask the seller to give you a demonstration.

Test the moving parts. Check the tuning pegs and make sure they are working properly. If the guitar is electric, plug it into an amp, turn it on and test the volume and tone knobs, as well as the pickup selectors. Listen for unwanted sounds like cracking or buzzing.

Remember, **all prices are negotiable**!

CHAPTER 4

First Chords

Topics covered:

- How to read chord diagrams

- How to read TAB

- Posture and hand positioning

- Basic strumming

A *chord* is any collection of 3 or more notes sounded simultaneously (when the notes are sounded individually we call them *arpeggios*). On the guitar, chords are played by *plucking* or *strumming* multiple strings at the same time, using a combination of *fretted notes* and/or *open strings*. The word *chord* is synonymous with the word **harmony**. When you combine **harmony** with **melody** and **rhythm,** you get music!

The vast majority of your time playing guitar will be spent playing chords, so the sooner you are acquainted with them, the better. Even if you'd prefer to only focus on *lead guitar* and play ripping solos all the time, knowledge of chords is essential and the best lead guitarists know and love their chords!

Before we go any further on this topic, we must learn to read *chord diagrams*. These easy to read diagrams are in the form of a grid which represents the guitar neck. The system is simple:

Vertical lines = **strings**

Horizontal lines = **frets**

Dots = **fretted notes**

X's = **unplayed strings**

O's = **open strings**

Chord diagrams tell you everything you need to know about chords: the name of the chord, where to put your fingers, which fingers to use (fingers are labelled as such: 1 = index, 2 = middle, 3 = ring, 4 = pinky), and which strings to play and not to play.

Below is a labelled chord diagram. Study it carefully as we will be using these diagrams throughout this book.

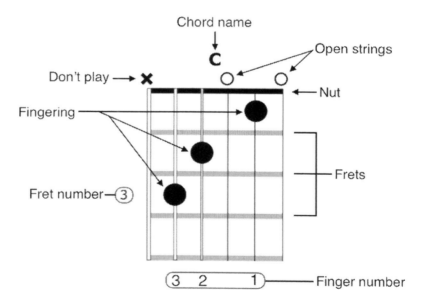

Let's break down the diagram above:

First of all, as there is an **x** above the 6th string, which means don't play it!

There are 2 open strings indicated, and 3 fretted strings, giving us a total of 5 strings in the chord.

The 1st string is to be played open (un-fretted).

The 2nd string 1st fret is to be played by the index finger.

The 3rd string is to be played open.

The 4th string 2nd fret is to be played with the middle finger.

The 5th string 3rd fret is to be played with the ring finger.

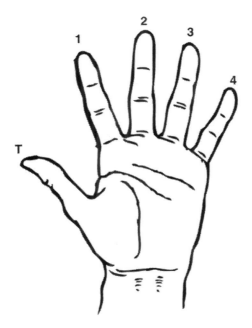

Fretting hand fingers are labeled as above.

Tablature (TAB)

Stringed instrument players like guitarists, bassists, ukulele players and even lutenists use a specialized graphic notation system called *tablature* or TAB, which depicts the precise fingering and placement of notes on the fretboard (as opposed to specific musical pitches and rhythms like *standard notation*).

TAB uses 6 horizontal lines to represent the 6 strings of the guitar with the top line representing the highest (1st) pitched string, and the bottom line representing the lowest (6th) string. It is basically like looking at your guitar fretboard upside down.

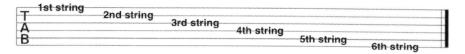

A blank measure of TAB, with strings labeled.

Just like the words on this page, TAB is read from left to right, with notes on the right occurring later in time than notes on the left.

Notes in TAB are indicated by numbers placed on the lines. The numbers represent which fret to play, with 1 representing the 1st fret, 2 representing the 2nd fret and so on. The number 0 represents the open strings, meaning you play the string without placing your finger on it.

You may also see music written in *standard notation,* which often appears above the TAB, but that is a subject that requires a fair amount of study and is a subject for another day! For our purposes, we will be using the minimum required to get you playing guitar: TAB and chord diagrams.

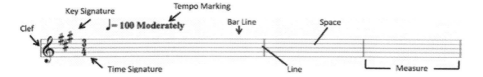

For reference, Standard Notation looks like this.

With that out of the way, let's learn some chords!

E minor chord

The first chord we will learn is the **E minor** chord or **Em** for short (a lower case **m** indicates a minor chord). This is a great chord for beginners as it uses mostly open strings and only 2 fingers! Take a look:

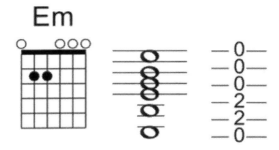

A chord diagram with standard notation (treble clef), and TAB.

To play the **Em** chord place your 2nd (middle) finger on the 2nd fret of the 5th string and your 3rd (ring) on the 2nd fret of the 4th string. Once your fingers are in place, simply brush your pick or thumb across all 6 strings, making sure that each one rings out clearly. Your fretting hand should look something like this:

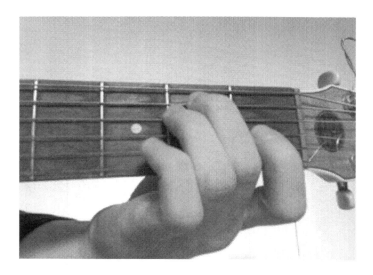

Note that the fingers not being used to fret notes are relaxed and hovering above the fretboard, ready to be deployed if needed. They are NOT tensed up, sticking out straight, resting on the guitar or tucked away behind the neck.

Here's what it sounds like played as a chord (all six notes at once) and as an ascending arpeggio (notes played one at a time, low to high):

Play: 2. Em Chord
https://soundcloud.com/jason_randall/sets/how-to-play-guitar-a-beginners-guide-to-learn-how-to-play-the-guitar-audio-examples

AUDIO EXAMPLE 1

PROTIP: When learning a new chord, it is quite common to encounter *buzzing* and/or *muting,* an unpleasant sound that we guitarist should avoid unless the music calls for it. Excluding actual physical defects in the instrument or strings (mechanical difficulties), there are 2 reasons *buzzing/muting* occurs when playing chords and 2 ways to eliminate them.

Problem #1: You're fretting the note wrong!

Solution: Fret the note right! This means you should be applying the correct amount of pressure so that the note rings out and placing your finger *right behind the fretwire,* NOT in the middle or back of the fret (read the section on posture).

Problem #2: One of your fretting hand fingers is in contact with an adjacent string.

Solution: Isolate the problem finger and adjust your hand so that it is no longer in contact with the neighboring string. Wiggle wiggle wiggle!

Learning new chords takes time, and *buzzing/muting* can be a huge roadblock, but by simply being aware of the cause and solution to this problem you can avoid a lot of frustration.

Okay, enough blabbering! Let's start playing some music!

Example #1 is a simple *strumming pattern* using an **E minor** chord played with all *downstrums,* with your pick or thumb strumming towards the floor (the opposite is an *upstrum)*. Strum the chord once per beat (quarter note) for 1 *bar* or *measure* and then *rest* for one bar. The example calls for 4 repetitions but for the sake of practice, play it as many times as it takes to feel comfortable!

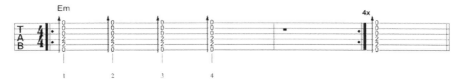

Ex. 1

Play: 3. Example #1
https://soundcloud.com/jason_randall/sets/how-to-play-guitar-a-beginners-guide-to-learn-how-to-play-the-guitar-audio-examples

AUDIO EXAMPLE 2

Not exactly Keith Richards but remember, there was a time when even he didn't know how to strum a chord!

Now that we know our first chord, let's try adding a bit of mojo to our strumming hand. **Example #2** builds on what you learned in the 1st example, using a lone **Em** chord, but busying up the rhythm by throwing in an *upstrum* on the offbeat of beat 3, giving you a strumming pattern like this: 'down, down, down up, down'.

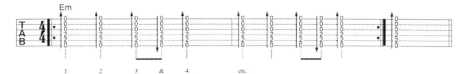

Ex. 2

Play: 4. Example #2
https://soundcloud.com/jason_randall/sets/how-to-play-guitar-a-beginners-guide-to-learn-how-to-play-the-guitar-audio-examples

AUDIO EXAMPLE 3

It's starting to sound like music, no? We could practice different rhythms over the **Em** chord until the cows come home but let's expand our harmonic vocabulary and learn a new chord!

The A minor chord

Another *open position* chord that you'll be getting a lot of mileage out of as a guitar player is the **Am** chord. This one uses 3 fingers and contains 2 open strings. Note the 'X' above the 6th string in the chord diagram, this means DO NOT PLAY.

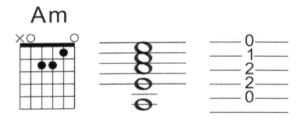

With this chord, your 2nd and 3rd finger assume the same position (on the 2nd fret) as in the **Em** chord, but this time you place them on the 4th and 3rd string respectively. Top it off by placing your 1st finger on the 1st fret of the 2nd string and make sure to let the 1st and 5th open strings ring out.

It should look like this:

And sound like this:

Play: 5. Am Chord
https://soundcloud.com/jason_randall/sets/how-to-play-guitar-a-beginners-guide-to-learn-how-to-play-the-guitar-audio-examples

Chord Switching

Since we've effectively doubled our chord vocabulary, we can start working on what essentially makes up the bulk of *rhythm guitar* playing, changing from one chord to another.

Example #3 is a simple 2-bar *progression* that alternates between the **Em** and **Am** chord. In order to concentrate on your fretting hand and making the change between each chord, the strumming has been simplified to 1 downstrum for every 4 beats (whole notes). Let each chord ring out as long as you can before moving your fingers to make the change, and try to move all fingers at the same time.

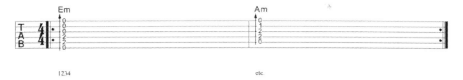

Ex. 3

Play: 6. Example #3
https://soundcloud.com/jason_randall/sets/how-to-play-guitar-a-beginners-guide-to-learn-how-to-play-the-guitar-audio-examples

> **PROTIP:** The example above demonstrates an excellent approach to take when learning new chords and even whole songs. By isolating each individual 2 chord change, simplifying the rhythm, and repeating the change until you can play it cleanly and in time, you develop your 'chord muscle memory'.

Once the **Em** to **Am** switch is feeling comfortable, you can start focusing on the strumming hand to give it some energy.

Example #4 features 2 bars per chord and one repeat. The strumming pattern is consistent throughout, but there's something new in the rhythm, called a *tie*. A *tie* means that one rhythmic value is added to the other, which in this case is an eighth note plus a quarter note (so it lasts 1 and 1/2 beats) occurring on the '&' of beat 2, carrying over to beat 3. This is a form of what is known as *syncopation*. The strumming pattern is: 'down, down up, (hold chord), down'.

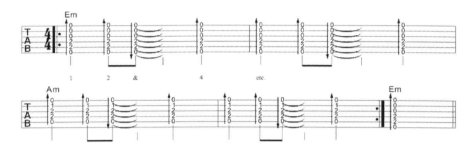

Ex. 4

Play: 7. Example #4
https://soundcloud.com/jason_randall/sets/how-to-play-guitar-a-beginners-guide-to-learn-how-to-play-the-guitar-audio-examples

Now, let's double our chord vocabulary again!

By simply adding a finger (in the right place of course) to the **Em** chord, we get the **E major** chord.

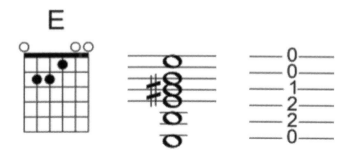

To play this chord, place your 2nd and 3rd fingers on the 2nd fret of the 5th and 4th string, respectively (same as you would for an **Em** chord) and then place your 1st finger on the 1st fret of the 3rd string.

Notice how this is the same exact shape we use to play the **Am** chord, but on a different set of strings?

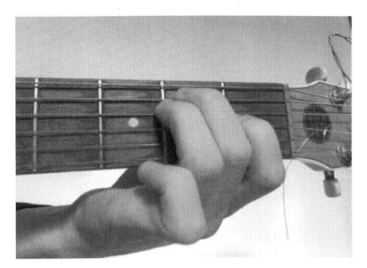

For our next chord, simply form an **E** chord and then lift your 3rd finger so that now the 4th string is open. This gives us an **E7** chord, which looks like this:

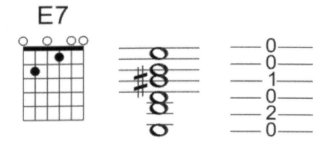

Now that we have some more sounds under our fingers, let's play a 3-chord progression.

Example #5 uses the chords **Am**, **E**, and **E7** and create a simple little chord progression that uses a 'down, down, down up, down' or '1, 2, 3 and, 4', strumming pattern throughout. To nail this one, try to move all your fingers in unison from **Am** to **E** as it is the exact same fingering, then simply lift your 3rd finger to switch from **E** to **E7**.

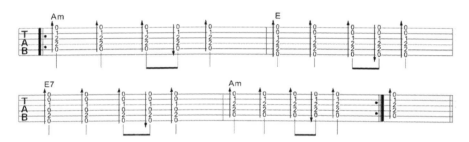

Ex. 5

A good rule when encountering songs with multiple chords is to isolate chords in groups of 2 practice switching between them until they are engrained.

Play: 8. Example #5
https://soundcloud.com/jason_randall/sets/how-to-play-guitar-a-beginners-guide-to-learn-how-to-play-the-guitar-audio-examples

> **PROTIP:** Whenever you learn a new chord shape, don't be afraid to experiment by adding or lifting fingers, or moving fingers around to different frets and/or strings, as we did above with the **Em, E,** and **E7,** chords. This is a great way to discover new sounds and may inspire you to create your own tune, or you may find chords that sound terrible, but there are no rewards without risk. And hey, it worked for The Beatles!

Getting the hang of it? Then it's time to learn a new handful of chords.

The G, the C, and the D

AUDIO EXAMPLE 8

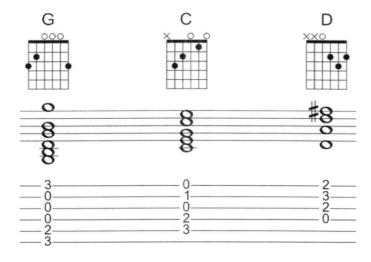

Here we have 3 important major chords that will allow you to play literally thousands of songs: **G, C,** and **D.** Though the **D** chord is rather compact in its fingering, you will have to do a bit of stretching to execute the **C** and **G** chords, which can be a bit tricky for a beginner. Take your time and you'll get it!

Here's what your fretting hand should look like when playing these chords:

G major

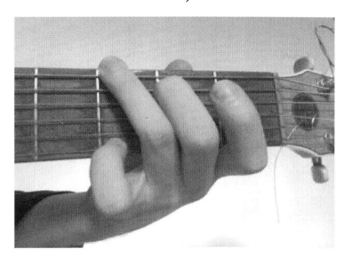

The **G** chord is typically played with your ring finger on the 3rd fret of the 6th string, middle finger on the 2nd fret of the 5th string, and pinky on the 3rd fret of the 1st string. Some players play a variation of this that excludes the pinky. Find the way you feel is best.

Play: 9. G Chord
https://soundcloud.com/jason_randall/sets/how-to-play-guitar-a-beginners-guide-to-learn-how-to-play-the-guitar-audio-examples

C major

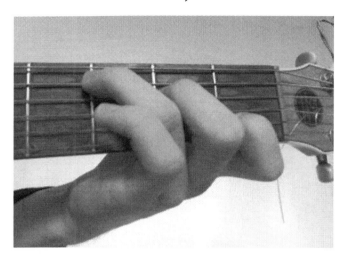

The **C** chord shares 2 out of 3 notes with the **Am** chord. To play this, simply form an **Am** chord and lift your ring finger from the 2nd fret of the 3rd string and place it on the 3rd fret of the fifth string. For extra practice, try switching between these two chords.

Play: 10. C Chord
https://soundcloud.com/jason_randall/sets/how-to-play-guitar-a-beginners-guide-to-learn-how-to-play-the-guitar-audio-examples

D major

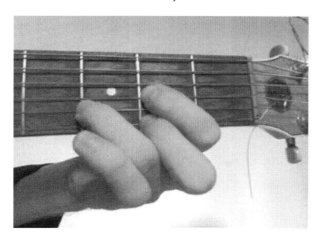

To play the **D** chord, place your index and middle fingers on the 2nd fret of the 3rd and 1st string respectively, and then place your ring finger on the 3rd fret of the 2nd string.

Play: 11. D Chord
https://soundcloud.com/jason_randall/sets/how-to-play-guitar-a-beginners-guide-to-learn-how-to-play-the-guitar-audio-examples

Once you get a solid grip on those chords and can form them in a fluid motion, you can tackle this progression:

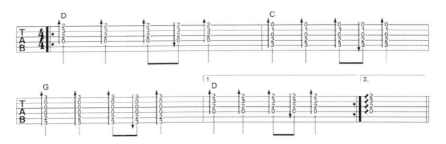

Play: 12. Example #6
https://soundcloud.com/jason_randall/sets/how-to-play-guitar-a-beginners-guide-to-learn-how-to-play-the-guitar-audio-examples

The strumming pattern with this one is a simple "down, down, down-up, down" but it is recommended that you start simply by strumming once per bar to get the hang of the chord changes, this is good advice for any progression you are learning as you isolate each part (in this case rhythm/strumming, and harmony/fretting) and then put them together.

You may also notice some new symbols above the music. In measure 4 there is a '1.' written above the bar line and in measure 5 there is a '2.' These symbols indicate 'first ending' and 'second ending' and you'll often see these in conjunction with repeat symbols (the thickened bar line with the two dots at the start of measure 1 and end of measure 4). Simply put, you play measure 4 on the first time through, and measure 5 (skipping over measure

4) the second time through. This shorthand allows for a less cluttered and lengthy transcription, which helps save paper and is easier to read!

PROTIP: Once you learn the 3 chords above, try and mix them up to form your own chord progression. You can combine chords in all sorts of ways, some more effective than others, for instance, try playing **G-D-G-C**, or **C-G-C-D**. As always, you should be experimenting with different combinations. It is very rewarding to discover cool sounds on your own and it's the first step in writing your own tunes.

Let's recap what we've learned so far. You should now know the following chords: **Em, Am, E, E7, G, C,** and **D.** Not a bad start!

This next example combines a few of the chords we've already learned while slightly varying the **D** chord we learned, making it a **D7** (see the chord symbol above measure 4). The strumming pattern is 'down, down up, up down up'. The chord progression is known technically as a **I-vi-IV-V** (1-6-4-5) and colloquially as the "50's/doo-wop progression", as it can be found ubiquitously in music of that era.

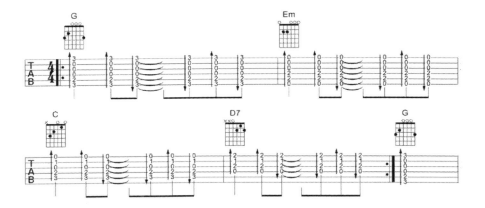

Ex. 7

Play: 13. Example #7
https://soundcloud.com/jason_randall/sets/how-to-play-guitar-a-beginners-guide-to-learn-how-to-play-the-guitar-audio-examples

We can take the same chords used in the example above and reorder them to create a slightly less dated, and even more commonly used progression that you've surely heard countless times. This chord progression (**I-V-vi-IV**) is often called the "pop punk progression", as many bands of that genre have made use of it. Its influence is far ranging, and has been used by artists like The Rolling Stones, The Beatles, Blink 182, MGMT, Aerosmith and even Eminem. Use the same strumming pattern as **Ex. 7**.

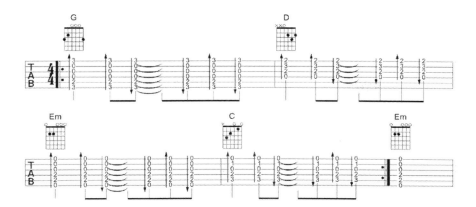

Ex. 8

Play: 14. Example #8
https://soundcloud.com/jason_randall/sets/how-to-play-guitar-
a-beginners-guide-to-learn-how-to-play-the-guitar-audio-
examples

Hopefully now you are getting the hang of chord switching and strumming. Beginning on the next page is a chart with the most common, and some less common, open chords (that is, chords that contain open strings) that you will encounter. You can try memorizing a few at a time (go slow) or use it as a reference chart for when you're learning new songs.

Open Chord Chart

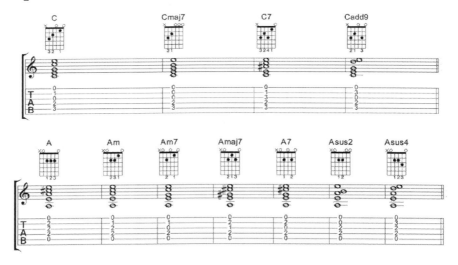

CHAPTER 5

Notes and Melodies

Topics covered:

- TAB recap

- Playing melodies

- Explaining the musical alphabet

- Note names on the guitar

The majority of a guitar player's life is spent playing rhythm guitar, and the instrument has a rich tradition as an accompaniment for the voice and/or other lead instruments. But the guitar is also a powerful lead instrument, and any well rounded player should be able to play melodies as well as chords. Most bands have at least one rhythm guitar player and one lead player (with a few notable exceptions where one guitarist plays both roles).

Lead vs. Rhythm

Lead guitar consists of *melodies* and *solos*, which are comprised of mostly single-notes played one at a time and in a particular sequence, while *rhythm guitar* mostly consists of multiple notes played simultaneously (chords), though *riffs* are mostly comprised of single notes and usually fall under the category of rhythm guitar.

TAB Recap

Before diving into single-note playing, let's quickly refresh our understanding of *tablature*:

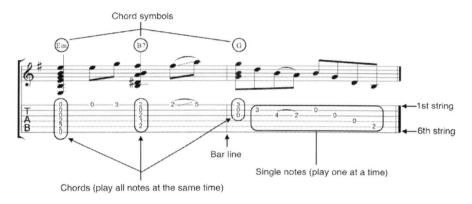

First Melodies

Now let's learn a few single-note melodies that you're probably familiar with. The first one takes place entirely within the first 3 frets of the guitar and uses the 1st and 2nd string. It's a little excerpt from the 4th movement of Ludwig van Beethoven's 9th Symphony called **"Ode to Joy"**.

Ludwig van Beethoven

Ode To Joy

Play: 15. 'Ode To Joy'
https://soundcloud.com/jason_randall/sets/how-to-play-guitar-a-beginners-guide-to-learn-how-to-play-the-guitar-audio-examples

Our next example is a well known hymn called "**Amazing Grace**" that uses the first 3 strings of the guitar. Note that the time signature is different than the previous examples (3/4 vs. 4/4), which in this case means you play 3 beats per bar instead of 4 (count '1-2-3, 1-2-3'). It is also worth noting the *chord symbols* written above the staff. These simply tell you which chords to play under each melody note but give no indication of rhythm, which requires you to be creative and come up with your own!

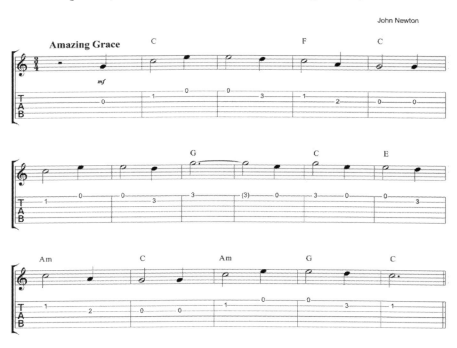

Play: 16. 'Amazing Grace'
https://soundcloud.com/jason_randall/sets/how-to-play-guitar-a-beginners-guide-to-learn-how-to-play-the-guitar-audio-examples

Here's one you can play many times a year for all of your friends. It ventures as far as the 5th fret on the 1st string, which can be a bit of a tricky stretch, but take your time and practice bar by bar, and you'll get it. This one is called "**Happy Birthday**".

Play: 17. 'Happy Birthday'
https://soundcloud.com/jason_randall/sets/how-to-play-guitar-a-beginners-guide-to-learn-how-to-play-the-guitar-audio-examples

Musical ABC's

The distances between musical notes are called "intervals" of which the smallest distance is called a *semitone* or *half-step*. On the guitar, semitones are represented by the distance of one fret, for example, on the 1st string, the distance between the 1st fret and the 2nd fret is 1 *semitone*. When you add 2 semitones together, you get what is called a *tone* or *whole-step*. This distance is represented by the distance of two frets on the guitar, so the distance between the 1st string 1st fret and the 1st string 3rd fret is a *tone*.

The western musical alphabet consists of 7 letters (from A to G) and is made up of a sequence of *half-steps* and *whole-steps*. Each letter is separated by *whole-steps* except for **B** and **C**, and **E** and **F**, which are a *half-step* apart from each other. Think of these notes as inseparable friends that you always see together.

In the diagram below, one octave of the musical alphabet is laid out on top of a ruler, with each tick representing a half step:

whole   half   whole   whole   half   whole   whole

As long as you know what note you are on and remember the "**BC** and **EF** rule" you will easily be able to find any note on a given string. The above diagram can be replicated exactly on the 5th string of the guitar (the A string) up to the 12th fret with the first tick being represented by the open string and each subsequent tick being represented by the frets:

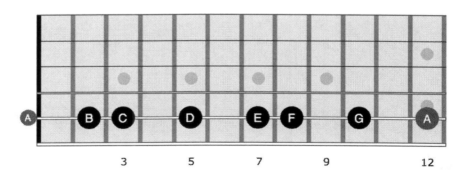

These notes (natural notes with no sharps or flats) are the equivalent of the "white keys" on the piano, and comprise the C major/A minor scale. For additional practice, try playing these notes on all the strings of your guitar.

For instance, if you were to play the 2nd string, you'd have to first figure out what the open string note is (it's B). Knowing that the next note in our scale is C, we then have to ask ourselves "is that a half-step or a whole-step away from B?" for which we know the answer is a half-step, which lets us know that we find the C on the first fret. Proceed on this path until you have these relationships burned into your brain and fingers, and you will be well on your way to understanding how the fretboard works!

Sharps (#) and flats (b)

The notes that reside in-between the natural notes are called *sharps* (indicated by a '#') and *flats* (indicated by a '*b*'). To *sharpen* a note means to raise it by 1 semitone, so if you want to find a **C#** note, simply find a **C** note and raise the pitch by 1 semitone.

C = 8th fret, 1st string

+1 semitone

C# = 9th fret, 1st string

Flattening a note means to lower it by 1 semitone, so if you want to find an **Ab** note, simply find an **A** note and lower the pitch by 1 semitone.

$$\mathbf{A} = \text{5th fret, 1st string}$$

$$\underline{\text{-1 semitone}}$$

$$\mathbf{Ab} = \text{4th fret, 1st string}$$

'Natural' Notes on Each String

Let's take a look at exactly where to find the natural notes on the guitar, up to the 12th fret. Beyond the 12th fret, the same pattern repeats itself until you run out of fretboard.

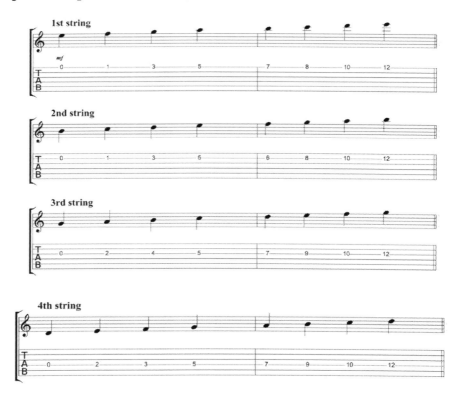

PROTIP: Learning the note names on the guitar should be a priority FROM DAY ONE! Take a few minutes to quiz yourself each time you sit down to play. Can you find all the E notes on the guitar? Can you name all the notes on each string? No is not an acceptable answer to these questions.

Knowing the note names will help you to be able to name chords, identify scales and key signatures, as well as communicate with other musicians and help you develop a more universal understanding of music.

If you've enjoyed reading this book, subscribe* to my mailing list for exclusive content and sneak peaks of my future books.

Click the link below:
http://eepurl.com/duJ-yf

OR

Use the QR Code:

(*Must be 13 years or older to subscribe)

Appendix: Important Guitarists

Here is a list of important guitarists by genre that you would be well advised to check out and have a listen to. It is by no means exhaustive, but should give you a good idea of the major movers and shakers.

Blues

Duane Allman

Michael Bloomfield

Big Bill Broonzy

Eric Clapton

Ry Cooder

Bo Diddley

Peter Green

Buddy Guy

John Lee Hooker

Robert Johnson

Blind Lemon Jefferson

Albert King

B.B. King

Freddie King

Huddie Ledbetter aka "Lead Belly"

Jimmy Reed

Hubert Sumlin

Derek Trucks

Stevie Ray Vaughan

T-Bone Walker

Muddy Waters

Johnny Winter

Howlin' Wolf

Country

Chet Atkins

Glenn Campbell

Maybelle Carter

Lester Flatt

Danny Gatton

Vince Gill

Johnny Hiland

Brent Mason

Buck Owens

Jerry Reed

Roy Rogers

Merle Travis

Doc Watson

Hank Williams

Classical

Dionisio Aguado

Julian Bream

Leo Brouwer

Matteo Carcassi

Carlo Domeniconi

Roland Dyens

Eliot Fisk

Mauro Giuliani

Agustín Barrios Mangoré

Pepe Romero

David Russel

Andres Ségovia

Fernando Sor

Francisco Tárrega

John Williams

Narciso Yepes

Flamenco

Paco de Lucía

Juan Martín

Ramón Montoya

Paco Peña

Niño Ricardo

Sabicas

Ben Woods

Fingerstyle

Tommy Emmanuel

Michael Hedges

Bert Jansch

Leo Kottke

Adrian Legg

Don Ross

Folk

Joan Baez

John Denver

Ani DiFranco

Nick Drake

Bob Dylan

Arlo Guthrie

Woodie Guthrie

Father John Misty

Joni Mitchell

Elliot Smith

Jazz

John Abercrombie

Tuck Andress

George Benson

Ed Bickert

Lenny Breau

Kenny Burrell

Larry Carleton

Charlie Christian

Tal Farlow

Bill Frisell

Grant Green

Ted Greene

Jim Hall

Allan Holdsworth

Barney Kessel

Julian Lage

Pat Martino

Pat Metheny

Wes Montgomery

Joe Pass

Les Paul

Django Reinhardt

Marc Ribot

Kurt Rosenwinkel

John Scofield

Mike Stern

Martin Taylor

George Van Eps

Metal

"Dimebag" Darrel Abbot

Mikael Åkerfeldt

Ritchie Blackmore

Jason Becker

Nuno Bettencourt

Vito Bratta

Chris Broderick

Glen Buxton

Marty Friedman

Gus G.

Paul Gilbert

Kirk Hammett

Jeff Hanneman

Matt Heafy

James Hetfield

Scott Ian

Tony Iommi

Kerry King

Alexi Laiho

Jake E. Lee

George Lynch

Yngwie Malmsteen

Dave Mustaine

John Petrucci

Chris Poland

Randy Rhoads

Michael Schenker

Devin Townsend

Steve Vai

Eddie Van Halen

Zakk Wylde

Rock

Jeff Beck

Matt Bellamy

Chuck Berry

Lindsay Buckingham

Kurt Cobain

The Edge

John Fogarty

Robert Fripp

John Frusciante

David Gilmour

Jonny Greenwood

George Harrison

Jimi Hendrix

Josh Homme

Joan Jett

Mick Jones

Mark Knopfler

Alex Lifeson

Johnny Marr

Brian May

Gary Moore

Thurston Moore

Tom Morello

Jimmy Page

Prince

Keith Richards

Robbie Robertson

Mick Ronson

Carlos Santana

Slash

Pete Townsend

Joe Walsh

Jack White

Ron Wood

Link Wray

Angus Young

Malcolm Young

Neil Young

Frank Zappa

Printed in Great Britain
by Amazon

17000722R00046